ADRIANA LUNA CARLOS

Editor-In-Chief, Designer and Co-Founder

HANNA OLIVAS

Managing Editor & Co-Founder

BRIAN LLORENTE

Designer & Editor

BECOMING AN UNSTOPPABLE
WOMAN

SHE RISES
S T U D I O S

ADVERTISING OPPORTUNITIES

Info@SheRisesStudios.com

CONTACT US

SheRisesStudios@gmail.com
www.SheRisesStudios.com

#BAUW

SHE RISES
STUDIOS

PRESENTS

Becoming an
UNSTOPPABLE
WOMAN
BOOK SERIES TOUR

BARNES & NOBLE,
MIRA MESA MARKET CENTER
MARKETCENTER,
10775 WESTVIEW PKWY, SAN DIEGO, CA 92126

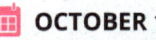 **OCTOBER 15, 2022**

4-6pm pst

Fearless on the frontlines...

Written by Hanna Olivas - SRS Founder and CEO

Women often face a battle in one form or another at some point during their lives - from figuring out how to feed the family to fighting to get the recognition, they deserve for their contribution to society. In fact, I would go so far as to say that women face the battlefield as soon as the alarm goes off in the morning - all for the joy and love of having it all while giving it their all. Wasn't it Pat Benatar who said it best - 'Love is a Battlefield'? But what makes some of us want to duck and hide under the covers versus the women who, without hesitation, put on their armor and own their truth?

Is it because society often considers women to be fragile, beautiful creatures limited by their physical or mental strength? Therefore some women buy into the myth. Or is there some subconscious fear of failing? However, deep down, we know that couldn't be further from the truth! Women are strong, brave, passionate, and resilient, and we power through life like a perfect storm. It is chaos, bravery, and beauty all in one. One of those women is Sarah Williamson. You may know her as the Aussie anchorwoman, living in Israel and left to venture to the big apple, NYC! She joined Newsmax as a journalist and news correspondent. You might remember her as the badass woman who went to Ukraine to cover the front lines of the war.

Either way, there is definitely more to Sarah. I was honored to interview this amazing woman and asked her to share some deep insight on bravery and powering through. I asked Sarah, *"What does Becoming an Unstoppable Woman mean to you?"* Her answer was so simplistic yet so profound. She said, **" Never take no for an answer!"** She shared how having no degree in journalism but having a passion for sharing people's stories is her duty. So Sarah became a self-taught journalist, from operating a camera to writing her own stories. Her passion for humanity is incredible. She describes the importance of being a woman who can power through no matter the obstacle or situation.

Sarah was in Ukraine for a total of four months and spent time with men, women, and children who were so deeply affected by this war. Some of them did not know when the next bomb would strike or where their next meal would come from. All the while, Sarah was there, bravely sharing their stories and helping their voices be heard. **She was there to bring out the truth.** She shared that she was never afraid for herself, but she was more afraid of being unable to help the Ukraine people and the daily tragedies they face.

I was so amazed by her heart and bravery, her compassion to want to help perfect strangers from across the world. **Under the most dangerous conditions, she stayed day after day to help whenever she could.** I asked Sarah what kept her inspired to stay there for so long, and she answered and said again, "It is Her Duty." Sarah felt the strength and inspiration from the people of Ukraine. She said she wants to return to Ukraine again. Sarah was the longest-standing correspondent in Ukraine. Her being there on the front lines of war was surreal. As I was interviewing Sarah, I kept imagining the fear, the chaos, the unknown.

I asked Sarah if there was one pivotal moment in her life that changed her forever. I could sense her reluctance to relive a terrorist attack she witnessed in Kenya in 2013. The Westgate Mall Seige began on September 21st, 2013. **A terror group called Al-Shabab attacked the mall while she was inside, and that was the day she thought she would die.** Sarah was held hostage for nine hours, and every thought imaginable raced through her mind. She describes the adrenaline, fear, and shock of not knowing what will happen. She faced the fact that she might not make it out alive at that point. It was then she chose to be no longer afraid of death. That day, four gunmen came into the mall with AK-47s to kill. Imagine the fear, the panic, wondering if you will see your loved ones again. **During the attack, 68 lives were lost.** Sarah wasn't given a choice; she had to make one. She did everything she could to escape alive that day. She has powered through some of the most terrifying circumstances in life.

We continued to chat, and I asked her, **"What is one thing nobody really knows about you?"** She laughed and said she's a pretty open book. But she did share that the only thing she is literally afraid of is spiders. " I hate spiders," she said in Australia. They are terrifying, huge, and everywhere! We both laughed, which was so needed after she described the Ukrainian War and the terror attacks in Kenya.

After our interview, I asked her what books or quotes inspire her. Her response was a quote, a personal one of hers: "If you aren't willing to do your job for free, then you probably have chosen the wrong job for you." She talks about having a passion for humanity and wanting to serve and help globally. Sarah says she wanted to be a journalist because she cares about human rights and people. **She wants to help people share their voices about injustices that have happened to them in life.** She will continue to help refugees, war victims, human rights, and more. Her platform is not self-serving by any means. Sarah is the true and purest form of an unstoppable woman. She is a leader by the example of powering through no matter what! Sarah, thank you for your strength and compassion for humanity. You will always have our support, love, and guidance.

You are a "badass."

the
INSPIRED & PROFITABLE
Mompreneur Community

WITH ANGELA BELL

Moms supporting moms AS THEY
START & GROW THEIR ONLINE BUSINESS.

@i.am.angelabell

MEET YOUR COACH!

Are you ready to meet your
Inspired & Profitable
Mompreneur Coach?

Learn More	I'm Ready!

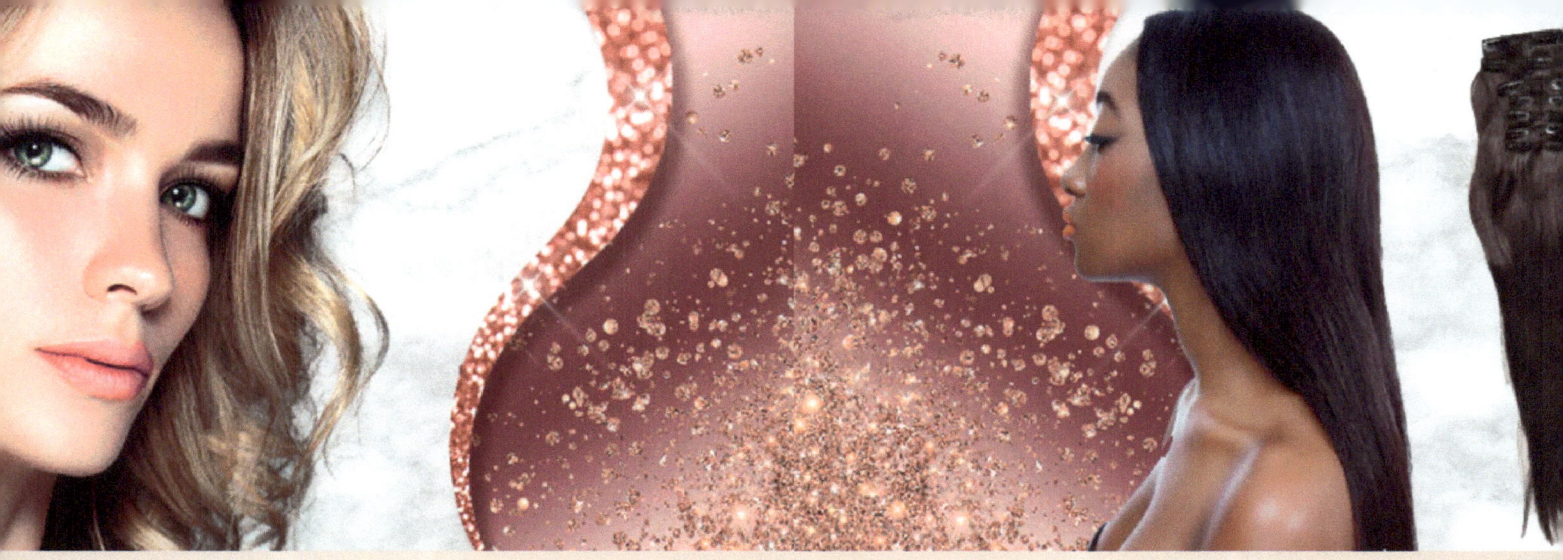

TOP QUALITY 3D LASHES

Have you tried quality 3D lashes? Once you do it's impossible to go back to the drug store brands.

CLIP-IN HAIR EXTENSIONS

The fastest way to add volume with a color that matches your own or try something new. Over a dozen colors of beautiful clip-ins available.

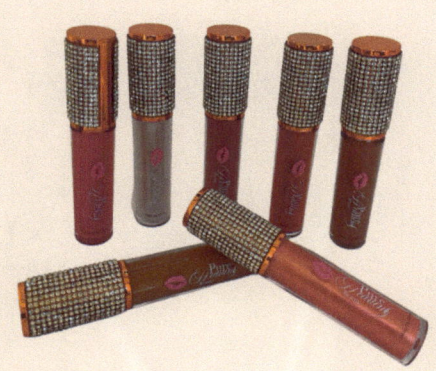

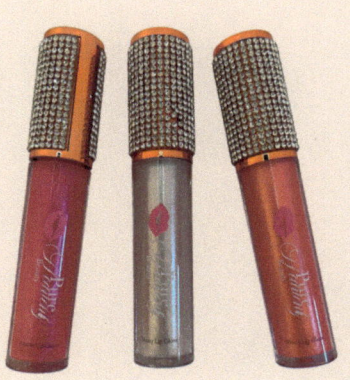

Where do we fit as women in modern society?

By Yudy Veras Bueno - Transformational Life Coach, Speaker, Author & Healer.

The fact that we are still asking this question implies that our place in society is still uncertain. We have made headways, but let's not become complacent - if we forget our history, we are bound to repeat it.

Only 100 years ago, women had no right to vote or buy property without their husbands' authorization. It sounds ridiculous - isn't it? Yet, it's a fact that we cannot afford to overlook or forget as we continue to gain momentum.

Growing up, I never felt like I had any strong women I could look up to as role models. At thirteen years old, I decided that being a woman was a curse. During my childhood and teen years, I dealt with a lot of unwanted attention coming from adult males who couldn't keep their hands in their pockets.

So, at thirteen, *I cut my hair and started to dress up like a boy to hide my female attributes.* Looking back, I realize that suppressing my femininity was a way to protect myself.

Today, women are empowered and unstoppable. Organizations such as Lean report that the number of women in leadership has grown over the past five years. Yet, - we are still massively underrepresented at every level.

Disparity researchers found that men hold 62% of manager-level positions, while women hold just 38%.

Nearly fifty years ago, we gained our right to choose - not long ago, in many states, we lost those rights. -There is a huge division on this subject, even among women. We had convinced ourselves that this is an issue of morality - When in reality, this is an issue of control - having an abortion is one of the worse things that could happen to a woman, as we are built to bring life and give life - yet, we as humans have the right to exercise our freedom over our bodies - whatever moral or spiritual implications, it should be a private matter between my creator and me - and it should not be anybody else's business let alone a few white men in Washington.

Even more scary are the statistics presented by the UN Women report; today, *1 in 3 women face violence in their lifetime*. 830 women die every day from preventable pregnancy-related causes. There is a lot of work ahead of us - yet, do not wait for society to change - you must be the change.

Our time is now!
We are unstoppable, and we must continue to empower ourselves until my last breath to ensure our daughters will inherit a world where our gender is no longer a sign of shame.
We must invest in our well-being and emotional/mental health. Only when I started my healing journey from the trauma of sexual abuse, rejection, and abandonment was when I able to embrace my femininity - I wore a dress for my book launch to honor my mother.

For the first time, I was comfortable inhabiting my own skin - I did not have to hide my curves any longer - I felt powerful as I walked into that room and picked up that mic. Yet, as we find our place, we'll stumble, experience moments of "disgrace" - we will make mistakes, and many will take those mistakes and exaggerate them to shame us - because power in a curvy body is threatening for many - We must remember all these women that came before us - they were unstoppable warriors - and now is our time to continue the job!

Let's do this, boo! - *Let's F%$*@% Go!*

Aileen Sicat

Spiritual Life & Intuitive Coach

I am an Intuitive Coach. I also label myself as a Tarot Coach, Spiritual Life Coach, and Reiki Practitioner.

I specialize in empowering people to make the best possible choices for themselves as they map out their path.

WHAT INSPIRES YOU?

Kindness and goodness humble me and inspire me. It reminds me of what truly matters in life. Even the smallest things can make me smile and inspire me.

WHAT MAKES YOU DIFFERENT THAN OTHER EXPERTS IN YOUR INDUSTRY?

I bring what I call my 'past life' to other industries where my logical side was utilized. As a woman of color from a conservative upbringing in a third-world nation, I like to believe that my outlook and viewpoint are from a wider perspective.

I also do not just give readings. I conduct interactive sessions where the output and sharing of the querent/client matter much for maximum effect.

WHAT'S THE BEST PIECE OF ADVICE YOU CAN SHARE TO HELP OTHERS BECOME UNSTOPPABLE?

Choose to be unstoppable each day. No exceptions. No ifs and buts. Turn it into a habit and into something you genuinely believe about yourself.

www.instagram.com/sheisaileens
www.rainbowswithaileen.com
www.tiktok.com/@sheisaileens
www.linkedin.com/in/aileens
www.clubhouse.com/@aileens

Tell us about your latest book collaboration in Becoming an Unstoppable Woman Entrepreneur!

My story is titled Stepping Out in Faith, which basically boils down to deciding to better yourself and then going for your goals no matter the challenges that will get in your way. By facing your obstacles, you not only empower yourself but also become unstoppable. In my experience, challenges and trials come as soon as you set out to achieve your big goals. Once I started to see these as a sign I was doing something right the magic started happening. When I help other business owners see this, I genuinely feel unstoppable!

Connect with Laura Croce

What has been one of the biggest challenges in your life and how did you overcome it?

Sometimes we are our own worst enemies. My own negative self-talk has been a constant challenge. At some point in my journey, I realized I am not my thoughts. My "Ah-Ha" moment was when I changed my beliefs about myself and what I was doing. Once I was truly focused on my goals and not listening to my own self-doubts (or the negativity from others!) is where I was able to begin manifesting my dreams.

Tell us about your current aspirations, business, or both! What do you specialize in and what fuels your PASSION?

I started my own coaching and consulting business: Laura Croce Christian Business Coaching & Consulting. I have the opportunity to inspire others, and I am blessed to get to see people thriving in their careers and in their personal lives. The more I serve, the more blessings come back to me, and it is such a blessing to see women reach for the stars.

I have an extensive background in real estate investing with over 30 years in the business. I am passionate about it, but real estate ebbs and flows depending on the market. Because of the fluctuations, I have time to work on my other passion: helping people start a business or improve their business. I also have a passion for assisting women in getting back on track while they work to overcome hardships like addiction and abuse. I teach bible study for women in recovery, and it is so rewarding to see these amazing women take their lives back.

LET'S TALK

Website:
www.lauracroce.com
Facebook/Instagram:
@coachlauracroce
LinkedIn:
www.linkedin.com/company/laura-croce-christian-business-coaching

THE SHE RISES STUDIOS PODCAST

Our vision is to build a community of women leaders who have overcome triumph and adversity while being celebrated, educated, and empowered to Rise Up in life and change the world! Join She Rises Studios hosts, Founder Hanna Olivas and Co-Founder Adriana Luna Carlos, as they interview some of the most inspirational and influential empowered women leaders weekly on Wednesdays at 9 am PST.

BECOME A GUEST SPEAKER

Share your message with millions of listeners WORLDWIDE! Inspire, empower, and connect with UNSTOPPABLE women around the world through the She Rises Studios Podcast.

Get featured on major platforms like Spotify, Google Podcasts, Apple Podcasts, iHeart Radio, Youtube, Pandora Music, etc.

Get in touch with us if you are interested.

INTRODUCING

SHE RISES STUDIOS
A C A D E M Y

The She Rises Studios (SRS) Academy is an online educational platform designed to help women advance their personal lives, careers, and in businesses through a series of relevant high-level skills courses.

Some of the things covered are:

- 🚀 SRS Author's Guide to Profit
- 🚀 Digital Marketing & Branding
- 🚀 Building a Business From 0 to 100
- 🚀 How to Achieve an Unstoppable Mindset

LAUNCHING NOV 2022

Secure Your **$24.99** monthly rate for **ONE YEAR**, by Pre-Registering TODAY at www.SheRisesStudios.com

Pricing Normally at **$34.99/mo.**
Discounted Rate of $24.99 a month is valid to the first 200 people ONLY.

The Passive Income PATHWAY

ESCAPE the WORKER BEE LIFESTYLE

ARE YOU TIRED OF...

Working 8+ hours a day, hustling to make ends meet, missing out on travel, family time and life?

As a licensed financial advisor, I am legally obligated to serve your best interests. In order to do that, I will ask you questions about your current financial situation. All your information is confidential and your privacy is protected by law.

I write a step-by-step financial plan to provide you with a Financial Journey Roadmap© so you can escape the worker bee lifestyle

I offer both one-on-one and group coaching, to ensure you always have the support you need to take the next step on your journey toward financial freedom.

BOOK NOW

www.SarahNicoleNadler.com
971-284-1442

HEATHER STOKES BENTON

Tell us a brief overview of your story and what makes you an unstoppable woman entrepreneur.

As a wife, mother of three girls, business owner, homeschooler, and caregiver, *I wear many hats*. Over the last 20 years, the adventure of life had its ups and downs. Leaving me in a survival mood many times. But it wasn't until I woke up committed to going from surviving to thriving that things started to change! Financial wellness, success, and mental strength are all choices. Once I realized I didn't have to simply accept what life handed me, what previously seemed impossible wasn't so hard.

What do you specialize in and what fuels your passions?

We are continuously evolving and changing. I told myself And now my clients do something every day that'll make one day in your future easier. Nothing is impossible, for, inside the word, it tells you I'm possible. The difference between surviving and thriving is from simple faith to actual belief. Believe you can and will accomplish your goals. Then Through strategic and consistent effort, you start to see change evolve in front of you. My mission is to help other families, women, and small business owners realize their financial potential. So often, we put aside our financial wellness and focus only on what's in front of us and said of what the future can be. We don't plan to fail; we fail to plan. That's why I started financial GPS. I want people to understand their financial path, to look at it like a roadmap that they have control over their final destination. Just because you may not have grown up wealthy doesn't mean you can't change yourself and your family's financial trajectory. I enjoy helping families become properly protected, financially independent, debt-free, and Traumatic event proof. With proper planning, when life has ups and downs, you can ride the waves instead of being completely wiped out!

HEATHER STOKES BENTON

What has been one of the biggest challenges in your life and how did you overcome it?

Accepting the life we had planned and worked so hard for was not going to be the same or anything like what we had thought was the hardest thing. Catastrophic events, injury, and illness I've taken away the life we know. Admitting that I didn't know how to move forward and I didn't have all the right answers sparked a journey into enlightenment and knowledge that I need it. I used creative financial strategies to take us from simply surviving to thriving; with our faith, we could change our mindset.

What has been one of the biggest challenges in your life and how did you overcome it?

Whether it's in business, motherhood, entrepreneurship, marriage, or simply navigating life, Becoming unstoppable to me means being prepared, ready, willing, and able. To be ready for something to go wrong possibly. Willing to admit you don't have all the answers and open to receiving the gift of knowledge from others. Have complete faith and trust in your path, journey, and goals. Then you have to show up; you have to be willing and able to be consistent, present and committed.

What's the best piece of advice you want to share with the She Rises Community to help them Become Unstoppable In life & Business?

The best piece of advice I can offer is to stop allowing fear to Interfere with your accomplishments. Find your reason or your why!! Allow it to fuel your drive to succeed. My why is my girls, and wanting a better life for them. Building generational change and learning more so I can guide them to a bright future.

What is another goal or aspiration of yours that you are working towards?

I have a lot of things in the works for 2022-2023. Aside from being a co-author of the Unstoppable book series, I am starting a new Business venture with two other amazing women. It is called "All Things Small Business" to help business owners just starting out or for those who may be struggling! We are starting a podcast, YouTube, and Facebook group to help support them. I'm also looking to expand into several other states with my Financial GPS business to help more families, women, and business owners accomplish financial wellness and stability. In addition, both my younger girls are on their entrepreneurship journeys. So, trying to help foster those hopes and dreams. Like I said, I wear many hats!!

What has been one of the biggest challenges in your life and how did you overcome it?

Whether it's in business, motherhood, entrepreneurship, marriage, or simply navigating life, Becoming unstoppable to me means being prepared, ready, willing, and able. To be ready for something to go wrong possibly. Willing to admit you don't have all the answers and open to receiving the gift of knowledge from others. Have complete faith and trust in your path, journey, and goals. Then you have to show up; you have to be willing and able to be consistent, present and committed.

Connect with Heather Stokes Benton -Financial GPS

**Licensed Life Insurance Agent
Investment Consultant**

www.facebook.com/financiallyfocusedfamilies
www.facebook.com/groups/490021218981192
www.linkedin.com/in/heather-stokes-benton-899624204

SUCCESS STARTS WITH SELF

35 Must-Read Articles to Set You Up For Long-Term Success in Life, Love and Your Career

One life-changing pdf eBook!
The three most important aspects in life:
Part 1: Wellness & Self-care
Part 2: Connections & Relationships
Part 3: Success & Growth

ONLY £37.00

+ Free access to bonuses worth over £400!
Visit www.divya-chandegra.com/courses for eBook offer and more.

@divya.chandegra
www.divya-chandegra.com

WOMEN IN BU$INESS

Amazon Stores – A Smart Investment for Passive Income Opportunity

By Gina Redzanic - Success Coach

The eCommerce industry is expected to grow by almost $11 trillion between 2022 and 2025. As businesses came online during the COVID-19 pandemic, the global trend toward digitization surged ahead at lightning speed. Even as regions begin to reopen, eCommerce growth keeps climbing. Naturally, I took a look, and then a deeper dive. My mission is to build self-confidence in women and help them create long-term wealth. I have had success in small business, direct sales, and affiliate marketing. However, when I read stats like this about eCommerce, I know investing in this space is a big opportunity to create passive income. Allow me to share with you today...

If you're looking for a safe, low-cost and profitable investment, eCommerce is the right option. Since there is no need for a brick-and-mortar location, the most expensive elements are quickly eliminated. Investing in eCommerce results in more expansion opportunities.

At the same time, Amazon's revenue and profits continue to soar, so do the opportunities for those interested in acquiring Amazon businesses. Over the past several years, we've seen the marketplace for Amazon businesses grow steadily with no signs of slowing down. Increased customer demand combined with a proven business model is making many Amazon businesses highly desirable among investors.

With over 2.5 million sellers and a combined sales volume of 4000 products per minute on average in the U.S., it's no surprise that Amazon's annual growth rate has exceeded 37%.

GINA REDZANIC

I had money set aside to invest and wanted to think carefully before deciding. After several months of research, **I decided to invest in an Amazon Store-** I was even able to find a company that offered a bundle—Amazon and Facebook "stores." As a busy mom, business owner, and someone struggling with my tech skills, I was not interested in doing the backend work myself. In fact, I wasn't looking for work, and I wanted a smart investment. There are many benefits to investing in an Amazon business with a company that does 95% of the WORK. Some of the primary advantages I found include:

- The marketplace has matured, making Amazon businesses a more stable investment.
- Ownership transfer is relatively simple and straightforward.
- Many eCommerce stores have an Amazon component.
- Amazon seller growth is consistent.
- There are numerous tools, resources, and agencies to help Amazon businesses succeed.
- No need to do your own fulfillment
- The backend team are all in-house employees, working for 100% commission (they only get paid when your store does well!)

I don't think this is a good investment for everyone. This is for an entrepreneurial or business-savvy individual looking for a "done for you" business investment. If you desire to set up a cash flow system, and you have strong credit and money to invest, then you really want to take a hard long look at this. **I firmly believe this is a BIG opportunity in this eCommerce space.**

There are some important aspects to consider. First of all, this is an investment opportunity; think of this as investing in online real estate. The initial 90 days are dedicated to setting up your store, do not expect to make a profit within this time. Be patient; after 12 months, many investors can see a 10k-a-month passive income or more! I stress that your income will also depend on your credit score and credit limit. In a more typical expectation, most investors can see a 3-8k monthly profit. The initial investment ranges depending on how many stores you want and if you want a bundle.

You can expect $35k investment for an Amazon store and $50k for a bundle (Amazon and Facebook stores) Lending is also available. You do need to qualify to become an Amazon investor as well.

If you want to create a long-lasting passive income with Amazon, I would love to share more details.

www.Ginaredzanic.com
ginaredzanic@gmail.com

With National Women's Small Business month starting October 1st, I have taken a moment to pause and reflect on the past years. The pandemic alone was a heavy burden for so many people to shoulder, and it is so inspiring to see how small businesses, by and large, have navigated and managed to come out the other side. In 2021, a study shows that women started 49% of new businesses in the US, up 28% from 2019. three times more people of color entrepreneurs also started businesses during that time, adding to more than 5.4 million new businesses created in 2021, setting a record in this space.

I opened Taurean Consulting in 2015, a thriving business in Las Vegas. I launched Catalyst Mastermind in August of 2020 for small businesses to come together to lean on each other and grow together. I love everything about my two businesses, though there are days when I wonder how I do it all while I am married and raising three teenage kids. Women will ask me how I do it and what are your routines, nonnegotiables, and secrets. I cannot tell you if the things that I do are anything mind-blowing, though there are a few that I stay true to for me to be able to do the work I love while also being the best version of myself outside of my professional time.

Expand the Realm of Possible is my tagline for Taurean and one of my personal core values. I am a natural risk taker. I work hard to make choices in my businesses that push the realm of possibility. I want to grow with ideas that are vetted and thought out. I ask myself if what I am deciding is me choosing to play small or big, what will the ripples of that be and then stand in my decision. I have trusted mastermind advisors and circles of women I meet with regularly to discuss ideas to identify my blind spots and let me know I am on the right or wrong path.

I believe in the Pinnacle model of an operating system; that which gets measured gets done. I coach and practice this methodology. These key indicators in my business tell me the score and how to make decisions on the fly. These need to be measurable and discussed weekly. When there is an anomaly in the number, it gets addressed at the moment and solved to move forward. Knowing these numbers across my business helps me check them off the list of things that used to keep me up at night or cause me to make decisions not rooted in truths. Know your numbers, measure them, and hold yourself and others to them.

The Pinnacle model also highlights the fact that we all need a plan. 5- 10 years out is too big for a small business to sink their teeth into, though 1-3 years of a solid vision that can be backed into quarterly rocks accountable to individuals or me in my organization is a way to build a plan and execute.

A closed mouth never gets fed; if I don't speak up for what I don't know, want, or need, then the answer will always be no. I believe in being curious and asking questions to learn and achieve results. I believe we all have voices for a cause and opportunities to speak up for what we need. Doing so also sets a great leadership example for those on our team that we lead and gives them permission to ask for what they need to succeed. Being curious leads to innovation and growth. Be curious with your teams and always allow them to debate you on ideas.

One plus one equals three, Napoleon Hill. I believe, at my core, in the value of a Mastermind. I know when I am taking the time to work on my business with other leaders, the power of innovation and thought is amplified. I believe every business owner should take the time to work on their business with other business leaders for a minimum of one month a month. This group should be about communication, vulnerability, connection, honesty, and accountability. I have witnessed business owners paralyzed by indecision, bad past decisions, and scarcity mindset completely shift after working with a mastermind for as little as three months. Commit to one for at least a year to see yourself expand the realm of possibility for your business.

And finally, make time for yourself and foster healthy female relationships. I recently attended a retreat where nearly 7 out of 9 incredibly successful, intelligent, and wonderful women said they do not have good girlfriends or female relationships. This struck me in my gut. Your health and wellness days may be going to the spa or taking a hike, or catching up on shows or books, though I believe that when women come together to talk, share, and lean into one another, so many magical things happen for and to us. It lifts our energy, reminds us we are not alone, and inspires us to connect as humans. There is magic in feminine connection that we really need to be careful not to miss out on. There isn't a time that I regret making dinner or coffee chat with other women. I am better for it every time, and I hope the women I share that time with are as well.

What I love most about women's entrepreneurship is that we all bring something unique to the table. We can give each other the space to be our unique selves in an incredibly supportive and collaborative way. I do hope some of these nuggets resonate with you, and I truly hope I can learn from you one day. The magic lies in us not forgetting to do for others what someone may have done for us to light the path for future women leaders to follow.

For More Info, Visit - www.catalyst.vegas

CATALYST
MASTERMIND
collaborative

YOUR PR PLANNER

Always here, planning your success story...

What is Your PR Planner

Your PR Planner is a boutique Public Relations and Communications establishment. The fundamental plan of **Your PR Planner** is to build and sustain reputation for individuals and businesses.
Your PR Planner works on the exact execution of our client's campaign vision.

Services offered

Full range Public Relations services
Communications
Content writing
Branding

Industries Served

Travel| Lifestyle| Hospitality| Food|
Beverage| Restaurants| Health & Wellness
|Publications & Authors| Tech| Edu-tech|
Fintech| Crypto |Art & Culture
|Entertainment|Real Estate|
Marketing|Advertising

Contact Us

Yourprplanner@gmail.com

YOURPRPLANNER.COM

CHARLY NIESEN

Tell us a brief overview of your story and what makes you an unstoppable woman entrepreneur?

I am not your typical entrepreneur, but that is what makes me so unstoppable. In my chapter, I share my lived experience, hardships, and how that all turned into creating the many opportunities I have now and how my hardships created these amazing opportunities. How priceless our stories are yet the value they hold.

What has been one of the biggest challenges in your life and how did you overcome it?

My goal is to hopefully soon start a nonprofit in my area to support mothers and children with child protection cases and to provide a safe environment for reunification. To teach life skills, and meet them right where they are at in life. I am a recovery specialist, life coach, mental health practitioner, and wellness recovery action plan facilitator.

What does "Becoming An Unstoppable Woman Entrepreneur" mean to you?

It means living my truth, stepping out of self-doubt, and living my best life. It means being able to laugh, share, and cry while knowing I am among friends that really care about me and value every part of me. It means you're an artist holding the paintbrush and it's your chance to paint the picture you want.

What's the best piece of advice you want to share with the She Rises Community to help them Become Unstoppable In life & Business?

Trust yourself, it's a strength to ask for help and that we are all in this together learning as we go. At times it feels like we may have failed and need to start over but really we never start over we are starting from experience.

Connect with Charly Niesen
International Bestselling Author and Speaker

www.facebook.com/charlyrose29

LISA SHEPHERD

What makes you an unstoppable woman entrepreneur?

I became an entrepreneur after my daughter was born. I had never really seen myself in a certain job or career. My university degree was in languages. After a job in sales, the editorial team of a magazine and a translation agency, I moved to the UK (I am originally from Germany) to work in digital marketing. The company I worked for was great, but after having my daughter, I just wanted the time I traded for being apart from her to be worthwhile. Saskia, the co-founder of Bloom Bakers, worked in the same agency and also had young children. We met regularly to bake biscuits and build castles in the sky. One Christmas, she emailed me to say she wanted to start a business. That the time would never be right. She was right. I was in. Within three months, we launched the business. The following five years were nothing short of amazing. We baked for huge international clients like Amazon, Fendi and PwC. All from our homes, at night, after our kids had gone to bed. It was only during the pandemic that we took a leap of faith: we quit our other jobs, moved into a commercial kitchen space, and took on three staff members. All of them are women, all of them mothers. It isn't always easy as mothers are still the main carers for children, whether they work or not, but we want to set an example and shake up the world of work. What makes me unstoppable is my passion for my vision.

What has been one of the biggest challenges in your life and how did you overcome it?

My biggest challenge has been not losing myself after becoming a mother. Not only did I set up a business when my daughter was eight months old, I also have no family support where I live and tend to put a lot of pressure on myself. All of that led to me becoming quite unwell. I had lost my way, almost abandoned myself. It took me two years, a course of anti-depressants, and a positive pregnancy test to come out of a very dark and deep hole. Today, I am a lot more aware of my limits. I learned (the hard way!), that they are right when they say you need to put on the oxygen mask on yourself first. It is still difficult to juggle family life with a fast-growing business, but I have a very supportive and hands-on husband and an amazing business partner who shares the same vision and has my back at all times.

What piece of advice can you share to help women become unstoppable in life & business?

My best advice would be to ask for help. You don't have to do it all by yourself. Get a (business) coach, ask others for advice and help, and later on start delegating and outsourcing stuff. The more you have on your plate, the harder to keep the goal in mind. Stay focussed, do what you are good at, what you love, what the world needs, and what can be monetized, and there is no stopping you!

Connect with Lisa Shepherd -
Spreading Kindness in Biscuit Form.
Entrepreneur, Author, Public Speaker.

www.bloombakers.co.uk/
www.honouryoursoul.com/
www.linkedin.com/in/lisa-shepherd-09bb2b20/
www.facebook.com/bloombakers
www.instagram.com/bloombakers/

HANNAH KLINGMAN

Tell us a brief overview of your story and what makes you an unstoppable woman?

I always knew I loved people and wanted to have a career that involved working with others and supporting them on their journeys. During my junior year of college, I purchased my LLC, officially announcing myself as a virtual assisting company. In the three years since then, I've found a love for marketing small businesses on Instagram and have built a team of talented and resourceful women entrepreneurs who help me support our clients. In the midst of getting my small business off the ground, I battled a global pandemic, stigmas around my generation, and the ups and downs of entrepreneurship. Every day is a learning experience and an opportunity to push forward. I'm thankful for how far my team has come and what the future may hold!

What has been one of the biggest challenges in your life and how did you overcome it?

One of the biggest ongoing challenges I've faced is my own personality strengths... specifically the "Futuristic" and "Competition" pieces. While these two strengths have molded me into the person I am today and made me an ambitious entrepreneur; they've also shown themselves as a weakness at times. I've experienced the feelings of imposter syndrome, occupational burnout, and not "doing enough" in terms of my own expectations. I overcome this challenge by having real talks with and opening up to my support system and always reminding myself that I'm enough regardless of the external factors of life. Oh, and having an incredible counselor/therapist to challenge my thinking helps too!

Tell us about your current aspirations, business or both! What do you specialize in and what fuels your passions?

Currently, my team specializes in Instagram marketing for small businesses. We offer done-for-you packages that take a holistic approach to the platform to build our clients' online presence and networks. I'm working on expanding our packages to include other digital marketing services so we can further support our clients and continue helping them reach their goals.

I am passionate about partnering with small business owners because they often have the same values I do... family, time and financial freedom, and helping others.

HANNAH KLINGMAN

What does "Becoming An Unstoppable Woman" mean to you?

To me, becoming an unstoppable woman means pushing forward regardless of what life throws at you. It means continuing to learn and grow and surrounding yourself with others who want to do the same. Always remembering that she is not your competition... you are. Keep moving forward! Take each day as an opportunity to become unstoppable, whether doing something to grow your business, experiencing something new, or simply taking a day to yourself so you can recharge and continue putting your energy into the world. It needs you!

Connect with Hannah Klingman

www.hannahklingmanvirtualassisting.com/
www.instagram.com/hannahklingmanvirtualassisting/

Great
READS

We're changing lives all over the world! Grab a copy of any of our Multi Internationally Best Selling Books ❤ ❤ ❤

Available at any major book retailer, Amazon and of course on www.SheRisesStudios.com

Looking to become a published author??? Email us at info@sherisesstudios.com

Hot New Releases

NOW AVAILABLE

Get one step closer to financial freedom by learning how to manage and grow your money. 29 financial experts joined forces to share their time-tested strategies, tips and tricks, personal stories, and more.

COMING SOON

This book is about helping women unleash their feminine power within. A lot of women are wrestling with so many negative emotions like fear, guilt, trauma, doubt, anger, jealousy, and are further held back because of people pleasing, excuses, limiting beliefs, and unhealthy habits.

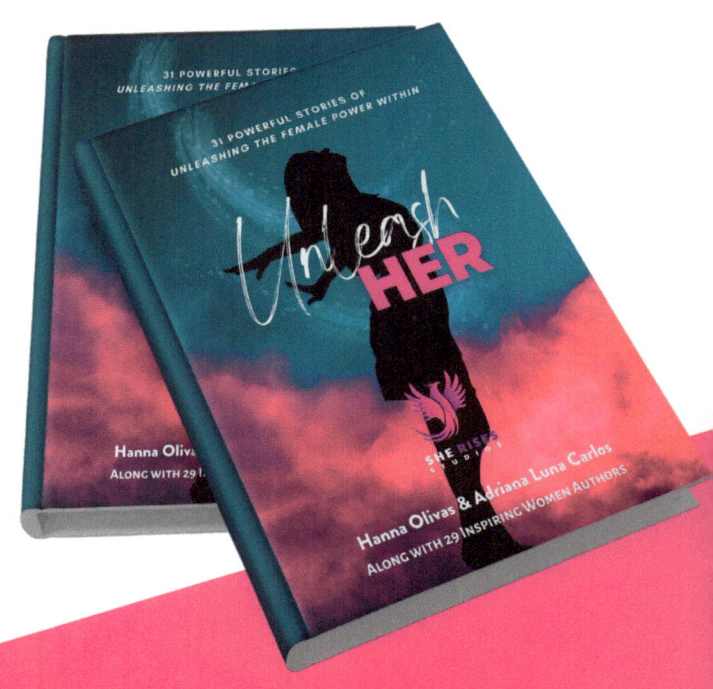

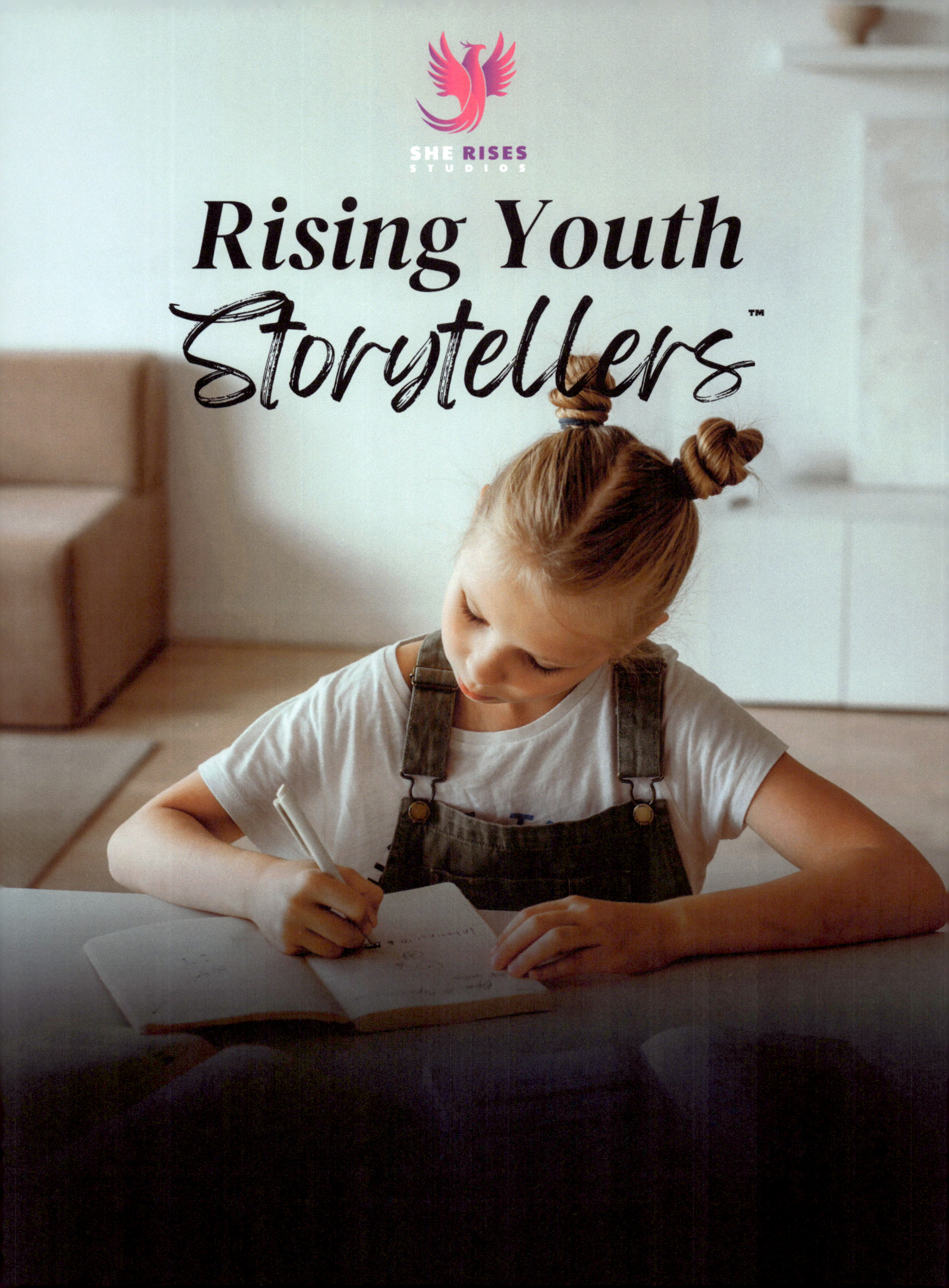

Rising Youth
Storytellers™

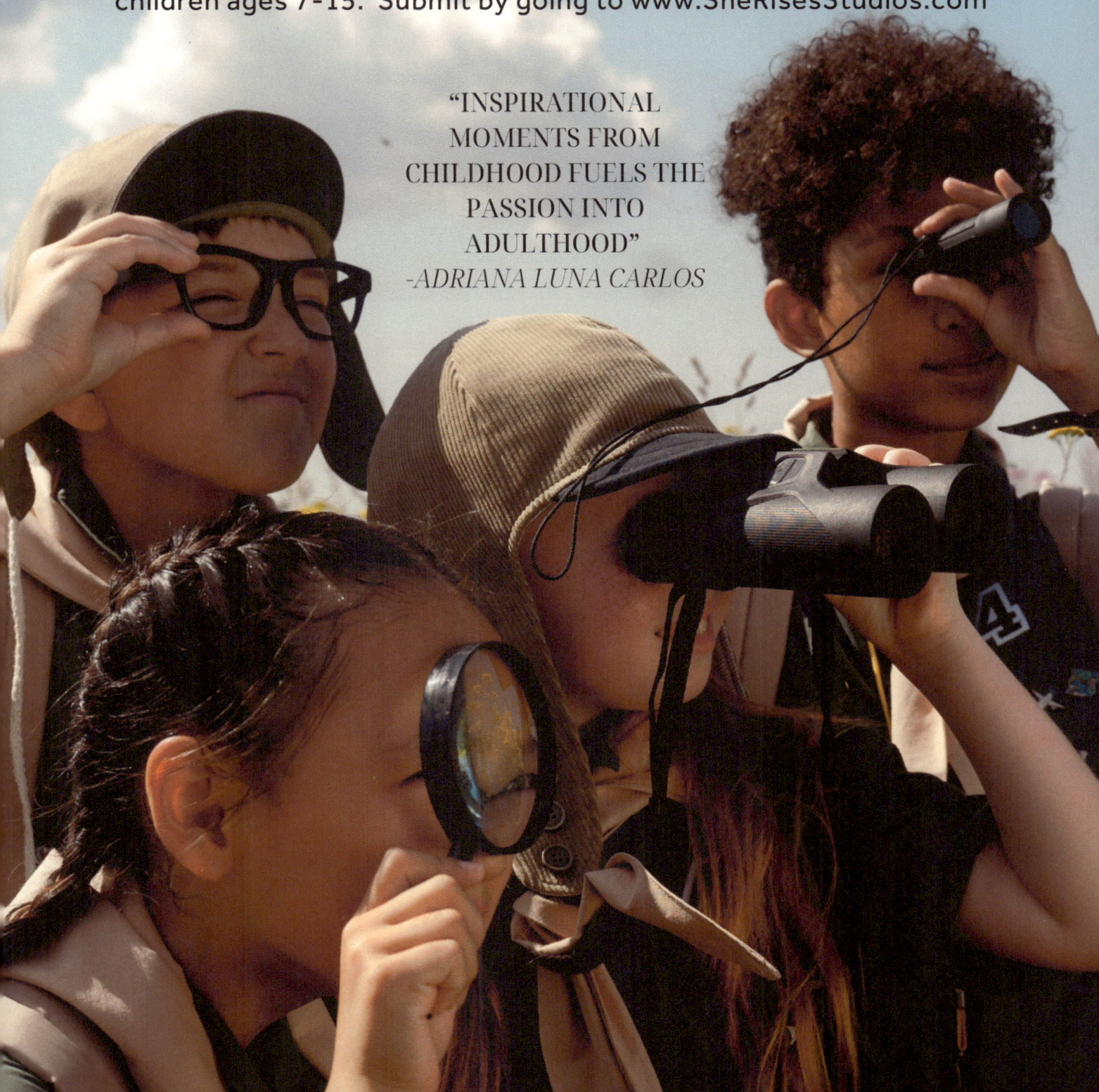

DO YOU WANT YOUR KID'S STORY TO BE FEATURED HERE?

SHORT STORY OR POEM SUBMISSIONS

The Rising Youth Storytellers™ is a new segment in the magazine where we feature 2-3 short stories or poems, fiction or nonfiction, each month from children ages 7-15. Submit by going to www.SheRisesStudios.com

"INSPIRATIONAL MOMENTS FROM CHILDHOOD FUELS THE PASSION INTO ADULTHOOD"
-ADRIANA LUNA CARLOS

MERMAID TRICKS

By Haylyn Benton

Once, there were two mermaids named Hadley and Haylyn and two pirates, Pirate Mommy and Pirate Daddy. The pirates like to trick the mermaids. The mermaids were tired of the pirates tricking them, so they had an idea to turn into humans and put on disguises, so they thought they were pirates too. So they went to the seashore and they found some…"human food!" said Hadley with excitement. It was some chocolate. Then, they looked for disguises. They got some seaweed, painted it with wet sand to make it look like hair, and kept some extra seaweed to show who they were. And they headed to the pirates' hideout. "Arg…Have any ideas to trick those stinky mermaids, Pirate Mommy?" Said Pirate Daddy. They had no new tricks to pull on the mermaids. Then they heard a knock at the door. Pirate Mommy and Pirate Daddy both opened the door and saw two Pirates!

The Pirates were thrilled to have guests. And the guests were happy to be there. So Pirate Mommy was making dinner, and she forgot an ingredient. So when she wasn't looking, Hadley and Haylyn put Hot Sauce inside of the pot! And when the soup was ready, Pirate Daddy needed Hadley and Haylyn's help with setting up the table. And they put super glue on the Seats the Pirates were going to sit at, and they put super glue on the silverware! Pirate Mommy passed the bowls, and she sat down. And when they went to get the silverware, it was stuck! "Shiver me, timbers!" Said Pirate Daddy. "I'll go get new silverware," Said Pirate Mommy, "I'm stuck on the seat!" The girls giggled, took some of the seaweed they kept, and showed who they really were. "The stinky mermaids?!" The Pirates were upset at first but then laughed with the mermaids. "We're sorry we've been tricking you. Will you forgive us?" The mermaids forgave them, and they became friends.

KAWARTHA ≈ HYPNOSIS

I LOST 90LBS WITH HYPNOSIS

Online programs available

Free Screening &

(705) 243-4925

Service Guarantee

www.kawarthahypnosis.com

Healthcare

Weight Loss and Nutrition

Share This Category

THANKS FOR

VOTING US

#1 FOR

WEIGHT LOSS

Platinum	Kawartha Hypnosis
Gold	Lotus Within
Silver	Rebecca Kerrivan
Bronze	Peterborough Centre Of Naturopathic Medicine
Top Pick	GoodLife Fitness
Top Pick	Kate van Gilst Nutrition

Voting 2022

Beauty

TALK TIME...

LOVELY LAGUERRE

Beauty Columnist

Do you often feel like your beauty products aren't working as well as they used to? If you're starting to feel this way, it may be time to switch up your beauty routine. Luckily, we've got a few easy tips that can help breathe new life into your beauty products and make them work better than ever!

Have you ever wished you could get your hands on some of Hollywood's best-kept beauty secrets? Well, now you can! We've rounded up the most effective beauty secrets you can easily incorporate into your beauty routine.

Trust us; these tips will take your beauty game to the next level!

Looking best is not just about wearing the trendiest clothes or having the perfect figure. A large part of looking good and feeling confident comes from taking care of your skin and hair. If you want to ensure that you're putting your best face forward, you need to start incorporating some of these beauty secrets into your daily routine.

It's time to say goodbye to dull, lifeless skin and hello to a radiant complexion!

BEAUTY SECRETS THAT YOU CAN IMPLEMENT IN YOUR BEAUTY PRODUCTS

Well, ladies, it's time to take your beauty game up a notch with these easy tips:

Go for a milder cleanser

For starters, ditch the harsh soaps and opt for a more gentle cleanser to take care of your skin. You don't need to spend a fortune on a high-end cleanser, but make sure it doesn't contain harsh chemicals or artificial fragrances. Chemicals that deplete your skin's natural oils may cause dry, itchy skin. One should look for natural ingredients like coconut oil, aloe Vera, or chamomile to help soothe and nourish your skin. Researchers found that washing your face with coconut oil can help to kill bacteria and heal acne.

Exfoliate your skin frequently

Exfoliate your skin regularly to eliminate dead skin cells and brighten your complexion. You can use a gentle exfoliator or a scrubbing brush to slough off the dead skin cells. Ensure you don't overdo it, as too much exfoliation can damage your skin.

Never sleep with your makeup on

If you sleep with your makeup on, your pores might get clogged and inflamed. Before you go to sleep, always remove your make-up. To remove your makeup, use a mild cleanser or makeup removal wipes. Don't forget to re-moisturize your skin afterward, either!

I like to use a sugar scrub or a gentle exfoliating brush once or twice a week. Dead cells can accumulate on your skin and make it appear dull, so getting rid of them regularly is essential. Beauty experts also recommend using a retinol serum or cream to help with cell turnover and prevent wrinkles.

Before applying lipstick, use a primer

Make your makeup last longer by using a primer before applying it. A good primer will help to create a smooth canvas for your makeup, making it easier to apply and giving it staying power. You can also use a setting powder to help keep your makeup in place throughout the day.

Keep your skin hydrated

Use a hydrating mask or moisturizer to keep your skin hydrated and prevent wrinkles. Choose products that contain natural ingredients like shea butter or cocoa butter, which are excellent for keeping your skin hydrated. In summer, using a light, water-based moisturizer is essential so your skin doesn't feel oily or greasy. Hot weather can cause your skin to produce more oil, so choosing products that won't add to the problem is important. Whereas in winter, a thicker cream is usually better to help combat the dryness caused by indoor heating.

Do not skimp on eye cream

Invest in a good quality eye cream to reduce puffiness and dark circles. Choose a caffeine-containing eye cream to help constrict blood vessels and decrease irritation. We usually forget to take care of the delicate skin around our eyes, but it's one of the first places that signs of aging show up. So, it's important to include an eye cream in your beauty routine. I recommend using an eye cream in the morning and at night.

Get enough sleep

The fifth beauty secret is to get enough sleep. It may sound common sense, but getting enough sleep is essential for maintaining a healthy complexion. When you don't get enough sleep, your skin can appear dull and lifeless.

Not to mention, you'll also start to see more wrinkles and fine lines. So, be sure to get at least 7-8 hours of sleep every night to keep your skin looking its best.

Choose the right beverage

Dermatologists say that choosing the right beverage is very important for healthy skin. According to them, one should consume a lot of water every day as it helps in flushing out toxins from the body. Besides, green tea is also said to be good for the skin as it is rich in antioxidants. Green tea can help in reducing wrinkles and fine lines. So, make sure you drink plenty of water and green tea daily to keep your skin looking young and healthy.

Enhance Your Products with Coconut Oil

Coconut oil can work wonders for your beauty products. Add a few drops of coconut oil to your shampoo or conditioner and enjoy shinier, softer hair. You can also add it to your body lotion to help hydrate and nourish your skin. Just be sure to use a small amount, as coconut oil can be greasy.

Setting spray is essential for long-lasting makeup

Makeup setting spray is a must in your makeup kit if you want your makeup to last long. It helps set your makeup and prevents it from melting away in the heat. Just spray some on your face after applying your makeup, and you're good to go. The best way to apply it is by using a makeup brush. Just dip the brush in the setting spray and then apply it to your face in a circular motion. The benefit of using a makeup brush is that it evenly distributes the setting spray on your face.

Love Yourself

The most important beauty secret is to love yourself. Always pamper yourself and give yourself some time to relax. Also, don't forget to take care of your skin and hair. You'll definitely look and feel beautiful if you take care of yourself.

By following these simple tips, you can breathe new life into your beauty products and make them work better than ever!

Your skin will thank you for it!

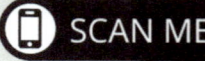

HER

AND NOW

The Art Of Connection In Business (Your Network Is Your Net Worth)

By Hanna Olivas - Founder and CEO of She Rises Studios

The art of connection in business is vital in building relationships for women entrepreneurs. It requires kind communication, intentions, and the value of the relationship you are trying to establish. It is a skill set all women entrepreneurs need to master. Connections in business are golden. Many women are unsure how to connect because we are stuck in a virtual world, and the effectiveness is not always there. So I propose ten powerful ways to make connection an art.

- **Lead With Confidence and Curiosity** (Introduce yourself, ask a lot of questions, and engage with your future connection)
- **Dedicate Specific Times To Maintaining Relationships**
- **Focus On The Right People Find and Build Your Tribe**
- **Use The Gift of Creating A Win-Win Situation For You Both** (Collaboration)
- **Be Visible To Your Networks** (Share who you are, what you do, and a problem you solve)
- **Start Your Own Networking Group** (Think about what is missing from the ones you are in and what you'd want to see and have in yours, offer value)
- **Become A Connector**
- **Don't Be Afraid To Be Human** (Vulnerability and transparency are critical)
- **Practice Practice Practice**
- **Practice Gratitude & Always Seek and Look For Inspiration**

By mastering these techniques, I have grown She Rises Studios into a global multi-media company for women entrepreneurs. It has been one of the unique aspects of my entrepreneurial journey. Remember " Your Network Is Your Net Worth," and master the Art of Connection. Reach out, ask me how, or take one of my courses.

Connect with Hanna Olivas

www.linkedin.com/in/hannaolivas
www.instagram.com/hannaolivasofficial
www.SheRisesStudios.com

Free Relationships Without Fighting

By Railey Molinario - The Love Educator

Tell us a brief overview of your story and what makes you an unstoppable woman?

Loneliness was the theme for Mental Health Awareness Week this year. Post-pandemic, we're recovering from the effects of isolation and poor relationships. I became the world's first Love Educator as I too have suffered from a poor relationship with myself and others.

Our ignorance of Love and relationship intelligence isn't our fault but rather the failure of society to well equipped us with the tools we need to thrive, leaving us disconnected and suffering.

I've realised how vital Love Education is for our personal relationships and guiding our moral and societal wellbeing. I became unstoppable in my mission to provide the world with the effective tools and techniques that most lack so we may become a more empowered society equipped with understanding, compassion, and connectedness.

What has been one of the biggest challenges in your life and how did you overcome it?

As an infant, I was abandoned by my father and left to sleep in the snow. As a child, I experienced abuse and neglect by my mother and stepfather. Growing up not feeling Loved left me in a critical self-sabotaging state. By 16, I left home to make it in the world on my own. I quickly fell victim to my lack of emotional and relationship intelligence. Determined to live a more purposeful life, I learned to become all those things I hadn't yet been.

What do you specialize in and what fuels your passions?

My mission is to provide the world with the teachings of relationship intelligence so that we may all become more understanding, compassionate, and connected. I teach the proven formula of achieving a happy and healthy long-term relationship in our modern-day world. Although my trauma has made me the unstoppable woman I am today, my work aims to give men and women everywhere this education without having to suffer as I once did.

By mastering relationship intelligence, we can master our lives. Relationship intelligence is the ability to successfully navigate our relationships with ourselves and others. Understanding how to manage our emotions and interactions with others gives us the power to live life in alignment with who we truly are. Anger, frustration, disappointment, and defensiveness are not emotions we readily choose.

However, they are present in our lives because we lack the skills to select an alternative. Through the art of relationship intelligence, we can live our lives with minimal negativity and maximum joy!

Connect with Railey Molinario

www.raileymolinario.com
www.raileymolinario.com/relationshipswithoutfightingmasterclass
www.instagram.com/raileymolinario
www.facebook.com/groups/224806782933794
www.facebook.com/raileymolinarioloveeducator

How a career journalist is now 'adulting' with 21 years as a self-employed publicist

By Ruth Furman - Founder of ImageWords Communications

Join a mastermind, they said. It will help you grow, they said.

I had no idea that joining the Catalyst Mastermind in 2021 would positively impact my day-to-day way of working, reacting and thinking. Like many businesses, my public relations firm badly needed a reset. I needed to grow up a little. And I didn't even realize it at the time. I'm going to take a few minutes to be vulnerable and talk about what the last couple of years has meant for me and my business.

Looking back, 2020 and 2021 were among the least profitable years for ImageWords Communications. Not because my work was slow. But because it was different. Even as the world seemed to be crumbling, I'm proud to say that I was able to meet the moment and find meaning in my professional life in a way that energized me and inspired me and even changed the way I'll do business going forward.

In those early days of COVID-19, a phrase resurfaced in my mind: "If you can, you should." While I watched businesses struggling, I knew I was uniquely positioned to be able to help because I have decades of experience working in public relations. Before that, I was a journalist. So I got to work, voluntarily connecting dozens of independently owned businesses with reporters for news stories. I helped a single mom who lost her job because of the pandemic and started her own keto bakery; a single mom who owns a cleaning service and shared Covid-related cleaning advice; a struggling restaurant owned by a couple with young children that pivoted to help families cook at home. I helped a Latina widow and mom who runs a Montessori school gets local and national coverage on all sorts of educational topics. I helped a mom of four who runs a mom-centered fitness business (which paused indoor classes because of Covid) connect with media and help parents with wellness and mental health challenges they were dealing with the shut-down and the era of virtual learning.

Altogether, I was able to help connect sources with reporters for more than 160 stories.

Of course, not all work can be pro bono. I also found a deep sense of fulfillment and accomplishment in helping my paying clients in their efforts to give back to the community throughout the pandemic. During an event called Paint it Forward, sponsored by a client in the construction industry, I was asked to help promote a campaign to paint the houses of families in need. Not only was I asked to help promote the event, but I also got to select the families, which included a cancer patient whose dying wish was to have her house painted and a grandmother caring for her grandchildren.

All of these experiences made me reflect on the way I do business. A reporter once called me the "godmother of the newsroom" because of my devotion to helping journalists tell good stories about real people—often who aren't even my clients. I've always tried to be a megaphone for quiet voices and a hype woman for the underdog. As I scrambled to connect reporters to mental health professionals, substance abuse counselors, small business owners struggling to hire enough staff, and parents of school children to talk about how they were navigating the pandemic, I truly felt that I was doing the work I was meant to do. Here's what I mean: When I reached my early 40s, I accepted the fact that she wasn't going to achieve my dream of having children. With a nurturing nature and a drive to leave a legacy, I decided to direct her efforts toward helping hardworking families and shine a spotlight on people who would not have had either the resources or skills to do it themselves. I also took on some mentees.

Looking ahead, as all of our worlds continue to evolve, I want to continue doing the work I was meant to be doing. So I'm shaking things up. Since I founded my business in 2001, I've operated on a retainer model.

I'll continue to do that for select clients. But to make my services available to more small business owners, I'm now also working with clients on a project basis, including both one-off projects and recurring. Because I know that many independent business owners have a limited marketing budget. But that shouldn't limit their access to stellar public relations and marketing services. I've always believed that everyone has a story to tell. That's what led me to start my career in journalism. Now, as a publicist, I'm honored to be that megaphone for my clients. Because every story could benefit from a little amplification.

About Ruth Furman

Ruth Furman has a journalist's curiosity, a publicist's enthusiasm, and a marketing consultant's strategic mind. Furman, the founder of ImageWords Communications, has lived in Las Vegas since 1999 and works nationwide. Her boutique firm has worked with clients across all industries, including retail, home improvement, design, construction, commercial real estate, health care fitness, and more.

A native of the Midwest and a graduate of the Indiana University school of journalism, Furman's background before launching her firm was in corporate public relations and journalism. Furman immerses herself fully in work that brings her joy and helps others, and one of her favorite mantras in business is "givers gain."

Furman has been a member of The National Academy of Television Arts & Sciences (NATAS) Pacific Southwest Emmy Awards Committee for four years. She's the only Las-Vegas-Based PR executive on the committee, which recognizes journalists annually for their work.

Volunteering for this organization has given her a deeper understanding of broadcast journalists' work. Ruth was honored to be named "Volunteer of the Quarter" by Nevada Hotel & Lodging Association, "Women of Business And Industry Award Winner" by Urban Chamber of Commerce, "Women of Distinction Awards Honoree" by National Association of Women Business Owners/Southern Nevada (media category) and she received the inaugural "Alianza" Award from the Nevada Latino Bar Association.

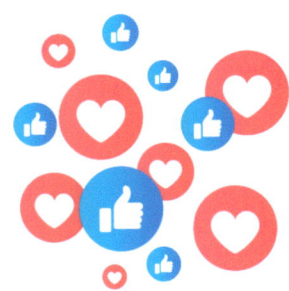

Connect with Ruth Furman

www.ruthfurman.com

photo credit: caseyjadephoto.com

The Power of Publishing

HAVE YOU EVER THOUGHT OF BECOMING A PUBLISHED AUTHOR?

WHY PUBLISH A BOOK YOU ASK?

There are so many reasons why someone would publish a book and we are going to share our favorite ones.

1 It can truly be fulfilling to share your story with the world, all while leaving a legacy forever.

2 It brings you Credibility and Legitimizes your credentials and experience within your industry.

3 You are tapping into a whole new industry, the book market industry, which is a $138.5 billion industry and GROWING!

4 It is much easier NOW than it has EVER been before!!! How exciting is that??

Here at She Rises Studios, we are striving to become the LEADING Publishing House for Women in the USA. We believe that the power of storytelling gives you the power to become an influencer and create a better community. We strive for growth, we are barrier breakers and are motivated to make waves in the publishing industry.

Get published with us TODAY!

Contact us at ww.SheRisesStudios.com or email us at Info@sherisesstudios.com

Let's take your business to the next level

SHE RISES
STUDIOS

We turn your vision into reality

The #SheRisesAccelerator program is catered to entrepreneurs ready to take the next step in their business journey. If you want to digitalize and scale up your business we're here for you! We provide support and expertise in web design & development, digital marketing, PR Outreach services, graphic design, and video production.

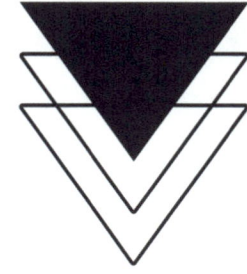

Web Design & Development

We'll work with you to produce the best web design that reflects your business' personality and objectives. We will design a fully responsive website that will drive awareness, generate leads, and increase revenue.

Talk To us

Social Media Marketing

We will help you turn social media into your superpower. We will help you create content, reach new audiences, and form a strategy that is sustainable and effective for your business.

Talk To Us

PR Outreach

Get featured in major publications, work with influencers, and build relationships with your target audience. We have deep connections to various media outlets and key opinion leaders that helps in making brands known to their target audiences.

Talk To Us

JESSICA BALADAD

Feel For Your Life

Jessica Baladad - Creator of Feel For Your Life app

"Get that lymph node, that big one," the radiologist said. He pointed at the ultrasound screen with a concerned look. I abruptly sat up from the table. "LYMPH NODE?" I cried out.

"Look, I've seen this before, and I'm pretty sure it's cancer. Meet me at The Women's Center tomorrow morning at 8 a.m." I didn't have plans, at least not anymore. Any plans I had for my life didn't matter. I now had to figure out how I would outlive a disease that had taken the lives of women three generations before me.

When I was 18 years old, I was in the shower getting ready for work and accidentally stumbled upon a lump in my breast. Given my family history, I freaked out and made my first gynecology appointment to get it checked out. The rubbery lump moved around like a marble in my breast. It sat below my nipple in the 6 o'clock position, and I could ping-pong it between my fingers.

When I showed up for my appointment, the gynecologist performed a clinical exam and told me it was just a cyst. She said it would go away with my menstrual cycle. "Great," I thought. "I don't have cancer after all." A few months went by, and I started college. While walking to class one morning, I noticed a pain in my right breast. I felt my breast under my backpack strap and noticed the lump again. Panic took over me. I skipped class and ran to health services on campus.

I gave the doctor a little background on my lump and my family history, and she sent me for imaging. After a few days, she called me and told me to come to see her after class. She didn't seem too concerned, so I took my time and made my way to her office at the end of my day. "Your results came back," she said. "You don't have a cyst. You have a solid mass." My heart sank, and I cried. She helped me call my parents, and we arranged for me to have surgery.

A month later, while in surgery recovery, I discovered that the lump in my breast was a fibroadenoma, a benign hormonal occurrence that forms in women who menstruate. I was relieved that I didn't have cancer, but that experience and my family history got me into the habit of doing self-breast exams.

Fast forward 15 years later, and I'm 33. I've been married to my husband for three years, and we're both career-driven individuals who enjoy travel, sports, and spending time with our families. We don't have kids but enjoy life with two cats. Every month for 15 years, I had done my self-breast exams. I knew how my breasts were supposed to look and feel. I knew my normal. I knew my routine and stuck with it.

I went to my appointment, and it was over and done quickly.

The practitioner didn't say anything to me about my breasts, so I went on my way. "I'm good," I thought. "I just went to the doctor."

But something told me to stay in my routine. "Eh, fine," I told myself. I went over the right side, and it felt normal. Then I went over to the left.

I noticed something as soon as I got to the three-to-four o'clock position. It was a dense lump that wiggled a little bit but didn't really move. I could move the tissue around it, but the lump stayed in place. I sat down in the shower so I wouldn't faint. "This is it," I said. "I have cancer this time." No, it couldn't be. I just went to the doctor. She would have told me about this. Right?

I was in the best shape of my life. I ran marathons. I lifted weights. I didn't drink. I didn't smoke. I was in great health! Breast cancer only ran on my dad's side of the family. No one on my mom's side had breast cancer. Again, the doctor never said anything about that lump. She would have found it and told me about it. Right?

I got out of the shower and went to Dr. Google. As I looked up my symptoms, I went down the checklist of items. No dimpling, puckering, discharge, bleeding, or rash. Just a lump. I thought I was good. All summer long, I kept an eye on the lump. It didn't seem like it was getting bigger, but it didn't move, and I couldn't tell.

The only other symptom I noticed about myself was that I was always tired. I would take long naps in the middle of the day and still wake up groggy. I even had to set the alarm in the middle of the afternoon, so I could make myself get it. "Wow, so this is what it's like to be in your 30s?" I thought. "I guess your body just gets tired, and you start napping all the time!"

I knew I had to get myself back to the doctor, so I made an appointment and saw a different practitioner. During that appointment, the practitioner asked me a dozen questions about my health and family history. She made a note of everything and didn't say much else. When she finished her clinical exam, she told me to get dressed.

As I collected my things to leave, a nurse came into the room and said she would schedule me for a mammogram. "Why? What did the practitioner say?" I asked. "I was just told to schedule your mammogram." When the practitioner finally came back into the room, her tone was soft, but I could tell she was nervous. "Is the lump indicative of cancer?" I asked.
"I can only tell you that it's a lump," she said. Then she began to tell me how her sister had just died of breast cancer, and she began to weep softly.

At this point, no one knew what was happening with me or my breast. I didn't tell anyone because I was currently in the process of losing a second aunt to breast cancer, and my husband had just started a new job. I didn't want to worry. I figured I would just handle it myself until I knew something for sure.

JESSICA BALADAD

On the day I went for my mammogram, I couldn't stop shaking as I stood at the machine. The imaging suggested they couldn't get a good look at my breasts, so they sent me for the ultrasound down the hall.

As I lay in that chilly, dark room, I thought about my husband, my family, and my aunt, who was dying. Would I be next? I don't remember much of what was said after the radiologist discovered the inflamed lymph node in my arm. It was the first time a medical professional used the words "you" and "cancer" in the same sentence.

My ears started ringing, and my heart began to race. I was stoic. I couldn't speak.

The tech in the room noticed I was in an adrenaline-phased stupor and offered to help me call my family. I think they were mostly concerned about having someone come pick me up because they were not going to let me drive home alone.

My stepmom met me and picked me up from the imaging facility. I called a few friends and had everyone meet at my dad's house. I sat down with everyone and told them how I had made it to that point. Tears were shed. Hugs were given. Fear sat in, but no one wanted to admit it.

The next day, I went to my biopsy appointment and brought an entourage with me. From that moment on, no one let me be by myself. In fact, no one would leave me the hell alone after that. Boundaries became essential. No longer was I was seen as a capable adult woman but a porcelain doll who was vulnerable to breaking.

The weekend had passed, and the following Monday afternoon, the radiologist called me.

"Mrs. Baladad, I told you during your ultrasound that I thought you had cancer. Tests confirm that you do have breast cancer."

I was diagnosed with Stage 2B invasive ductal carcinoma. The tumor was 4.2 centimeters, and I had five lymph nodes removed with my treatment. I underwent 16 rounds of chemotherapy, a double mastectomy, 24 rounds of radiation, and a 10-hour flap reconstruction.

My experience with breast cancer has driven a passion in me to help other women advocate for themselves, so I created a free app to show women how to do self-breast exams, track and monitor their progress, and set reminders. It's called Feel For Your Life, and I use it to educate women about getting screened, talk to their physicians about their genetic disposition to cancer, discuss the importance of breast density and show women how to take risk-reducing measures against breast cancer.

The app went viral in 2021 and reached tens of thousands of women worldwide. And since then, I have started getting messages from those who were learning how to do self-breast exams.

I got DMs from women who were getting mammograms for the first time. I even heard from one woman who discovered a breast lump that turned out to be early-stage cancer, and she's since made a full recovery!

Knowing that has made everything worth it.

As I continue to connect with women, I often hear about their poor experiences with medical providers and insurance companies. I've since started conversations to bring awareness to medical gaslighting, negotiating medical bills, picking the right insurance company for you, and multiple topics that encompass medical and patient advocacy as they relate to breast health. So for October, I'm launching The BREAST Method, an easy 6-step process that uses the word "breast" as an acronym to show women how to take control of their health and advocate for themselves. I started this project to make a greater impact on women's health and to raise funds for the National Breast Cancer Foundation, two things I'm deeply passionate about.

After my diagnosis, I later found out that my original practitioner did, in fact, find a lump in my breast during my clinical exam in March of 2018. But she said that she didn't tell me about the lump because she thought I was too young to get cancer.

Plot twist: I wasn't.

I never thought I'd find my purpose from a disease that has taken so much from me, but my work through Feel For Your Life is my way of getting my life back and giving back to others.

You can learn more about Jessica, the Feel For Your Life app, and The BREAST Method at www.feelforyourlife.com.

The Feel For You Life App

Available in the App Store and Google Play Store, the Feel For Your Life app is a free resource allows you to set reminders, helps you track your progress and lets you join a private support community. It's the first of its kind created by a breast cancer survivor who found a malignant lump while doing a self breast exam.